THE NEED TO KNOW LIBRARY™

EVERYTHING YOU NEED TO KNOW ABOUT

SUICIDE AND SELF-HARM

ERIN PACK-JORDAN

Rosen
YA
New York

To SBN. It's still your turn.

Published in 2019 by The Rosen Publishing Group, Inc.
29 East 21st Street, New York, NY 10010

Library of Congress Cataloging-in-Publication Data

Names: Pack-Jordan, Erin, author.
Title: Everything you need to know about suicide and self-harm / Erin Pack-Jordan.
Description: New York : Rosen YA, 2019. | Series: The need to know library | Audience: Grades 7–12. | Includes bibliographical references and index.
Identifiers: LCCN 2018010333| ISBN 9781508183556 (library bound) | ISBN 9781508183549 (pbk.)
Subjects: LCSH: Teenagers—Suicidal behavior—Juvenile litera-ture. | Suicide—Prevention—Juvenile literature. | Self-destructive behavior—Juvenile literature. | Self-mutilation—Juvenile literature. | Depression in adolescence—Juvenile literature. | Teenagers—Mental health—Juvenile literature.
Classification: LCC HV6546 .P28 2019 | DDC 616.85/744500835—dc23
LC record available at https://lccn.loc.gov/2018010333

Manufactured in the United States of America

CONTENTS

INTRODUCTION

On December 30, 2016, Katelyn Nicole Davis shocked the world when she live-streamed her suicide. The twelve-year-old girl from Georgia had been bullied and experienced depression. She had also engaged in self-harm, cutting her arms and thighs. Katelyn was active on social media and used it as a platform to speak out against bullying, encouraging other kids to be strong in the face of bullies. In the end, however, Katelyn did not get the help she needed and she took her own life.

Katelyn's tragic story sheds light on an issue that affects thousands of children and teens. According to the Centers for Disease Control and Prevention, suicide is one of the top five causes of death for teens. Thousands more teens engage in self-harm. According to Healthy Place, one in five women and one in seven men self-injure every year, and 90 percent of them begin self-harming when they are in their teens. More than forty thousand people die by suicide each year in the United States, according to the National Institute of Mental Health (NIMH). Not everyone who self-harms wants to kill herself, but self-harm in itself is a dangerous condition that requires treatment.

One of the primary reasons why teens self-harm and commit suicide is depression. Depression is extremely common. According to the NIMH, about sixteen million Americans will have some sort of depressive episode

Depression is an extremely common illness. Although many different groups of people experience depression, teens can be more susceptible to this mental illness than adults.

each year. There is no single cause of depression. Some people are genetically predisposed to depression, while other people become depressed due to traumas or stresses in their daily lives.

Certain groups of people are more prone to depression than others. According to a 2014 article in Medical Daily, these groups include LGBTQ people, teens with families in the military, military veterans, creative people, and introverts. Statistically, women, people of color, divorced people, people with no higher than a high school education, and people over the age of forty-five are more likely to suffer from major depression. But depression can impact the lives of people from all backgrounds.

Even though so many people experience depression, it's still a taboo topic that many people are uncomfortable talking about. Some people are afraid they'll be labeled and stigmatized because of their mental health issues. Others are afraid to talk about their personal issues. Many people suffer through their depression in silence, not telling anyone, not even a mental health professional.

If you or someone you know is suffering from depression, engaging in self-harm, or having suicidal thoughts, the most important thing is to find help. According to the Ganley Foundation, 80 to 90 percent of people with depression respond positively to treatment. The majority of people with depression do find relief through therapy, medication, or a combination of both. The most dangerous thing is when people with depression do not seek out the help they need. By recognizing the signs of depression, self-harm, and suicide, you could potentially save a life. It might even be your own.

CHAPTER ONE

DEALING WITH DEPRESSION

While not all people with depression engage in self-harm or have suicidal thoughts, most people who engage in self-harm or have suicidal thoughts have symptoms of clinical depression. Depression is a condition that impacts millions of Americans every year. But even though it's so common, it is still a taboo subject that many people don't like to talk about. This silence around depression can lead people to think they're "weird" for feeling depressed, and it perpetuates the stigma surrounding the condition.

When depression is acknowledged, it can usually be treated effectively. Many people who suffer from clinical depression are able to go through life functioning normally if they seek out treatment for their depression and keep it under control. The key is recognizing the signs of depression and not being afraid to seek help. When left untreated, depression is likely to become more dangerous.

WHY DO PEOPLE GET DEPRESSED?

Depression can be caused by a number of different things, and it varies from person to person. Some people get depressed for genetic reasons, because it's in their family history and they are predisposed to it. Others can become depressed as the result of a major life event, such as the death of a loved one. Some people experience depression as a result of life situations, such as living in poverty, being abused, or being marginalized because of their sexuality, gender identity, race, or another aspect of their identity. New parents may suffer from postpartum depression after giving birth, and many people experience seasonal affective disorder (SAD), meaning they often feel depressed during the winter months.

Sometimes, depression is caused by a traumatic brain injury or a concussion, which leads to changes in the brain. An intense illness can also be responsible for the onset of a depressive episode. Teens can be especially prone to developing depression because of intense hormonal changes and life events.

Some people have occasional bouts of depression, while others suffer from depression on an ongoing basis. If depression lasts for more than two years, it is called persistent depressive disorder. Other people suffer from bipolar disorder, which means they go through cycles of depression interspersed with extreme highs during manic episodes.

The bottom line is that depression can be caused or triggered by several different things, and it looks different from person to person. This is why getting the right kind of help for depression is important—different types of depression require different courses of treatment.

SIGNS OF DEPRESSION

Depression is a sneaky illness that can be hard to diagnose. That being said, there are a few key symptoms that are common in depressed people. Not everyone with depression will show all of these symptoms, but if you notice these symptoms in yourself or a loved one, consider that it might be depression.

- **Sudden change in mood or personality.** If a usually cheerful friend is suddenly quiet or withdrawn, it could mean that she is experiencing depression. Any sudden changes in personality should be taken seriously.
- **Losing control of one's temper over minor things.** Getting angry about small things that don't really matter can be a sign of depression. A person may be irritable or moody all of a sudden.
- **Sudden loss of interest in activities or things.** If a person usually loves going to dance class or playing a sport but suddenly shows no interest in those things, this could be a sign of depression. It is not typical to go from loving something one day to hating it the next.

- **Sleeping too much or too little.** Insomnia (being unable to get to sleep) and hypersomnia (sleeping for unusually long periods) are two sides of the same coin. These are both major symptoms of depression. Sleeping too much or too little can also be a sign of underlying physical health problems.
- **Eating much more or less than normal.** Sometimes, eating too little or eating too much can lead to serious eating disorders, such as anorexia, bulimia, or binge-eating disorder. People with depression can sometimes neglect regular personal care habits, like eating healthy and proportionate meals.
- **Having a hard time making formerly easy choices.** A lack of confidence when it comes to everyday choices can be an indication of depression.

WHO GETS DEPRESSED?

The World Health Organization estimates that depression is the leading cause of disability in the world, and it is the most common mental illness. According to the NIMH, about sixteen million Americans suffer from depression. Certain groups of people are particularly prone to depression. Those with a family history of depression or those who have suffered trauma or abuse are more likely to suffer from it.

Sometimes, depression can show itself through physical symptoms. Feeling unmotivated and tired all the time can be a sign of depression.

Overall, women and people over the age of forty-five are more likely to suffer from major depression. People of color and those with no higher than a high school education, who often suffer from economic stresses, also report higher levels of depression. Other groups prone to depression include divorced people, LGBTQ people, teens with families in the military, military veterans, creative people, and introverts. However, depression can impact people of all races, ages, and backgrounds.

Musician Demi Lovato has been outspoken about her experiences with depression and mental illness.

CELEBRITIES WITH DEPRESSION

The stigma surrounding mental health and depression makes it hard for people to talk openly about their depression, but a number of high-profile celebrities have helped to address this stigma by talking openly about their own struggles with depression.

- **Kristen Bell, actor.** Bell was diagnosed with depression and anxiety as a teenager. Her mom was supportive, and she was able to get help. In an interview with journalist Sam Jones, Bell stated, "I got on a prescription when I was really young to help with my depression and anxiety, and I still take it today."

- **Chris Evans, actor.** Captain America himself has experienced depression for many years. According to Evans, his depression stems mostly from social anxiety.

- **Demi Lovato, musician.** In 2015, Lovato told People magazine:

  I think it's important that people no longer look at mental illness as something taboo to talk about. It's something that's extremely common. One in five adults has a mental illness, so basically everyone is essentially connected to this problem and this epidemic.

- **J. K. Rowling, author of the Harry Potter series.** While talking with Oprah Winfrey, Rowling described her depression in detail:

  Clinical depression is a terrible place to be. Between twenty-five and twenty-eight was a dark time [for me]. It's that absence of feeling and even the hope that you can get better. It's difficult to describe to someone who's never been there, because it's not sadness. Sadness is not a bad thing—to cry and to feel. Depression is that really hollowed-out feeling."

THE STIGMA OF DEPRESSION

Even though depression is so common, many people are still ashamed to get help for their depression. They may feel shame, guilt, or embarrassment when they experience depressive episodes. Many people with depression do not reveal their condition to coworkers, classmates, or even close friends for fear of being viewed as unreliable, sad, or lazy.

Although progress has been made in terms of how society perceives depression, the causes of depression are still widely misunderstood. Some people continue to believe that depression is simply an issue of "mind over matter"—a weakness that can be overcome. Although research has shown that depression is a mental illness, many people are still judgmental when it comes to mental health.

In 1990, Mental Health Awareness Week was established by the US government in recognition of the need for more education around mental health conditions. During the first full week of October every year, nonprofits, community groups, and educational establishments around the country work to raise awareness about the causes, impacts, and commonness of mental illnesses such as depression, bipolar disorder, and schizophrenia.

These types of educational campaigns help to ease the stigma surrounding mental health issues. By learning about depression, listening to people with depression, and realizing that mental illnesses are valid medical issues, more people are coming to understand how important it is to get the proper treatment for depression.

TREATING DEPRESSION

Depression is a medical condition that needs professional help. Although depression is easily treated, it doesn't go away on its own. People experiencing

People who are suffering from depression often have a hard time functioning in daily life. This can result in poor grades at school.

depression should make sure their health care provider knows about it. Depression, when left untreated, can result in physical symptoms like fatigue, and it can sometimes lead to self-harm and suicide.

The two most common types of treatment for depression are talk therapy with a counselor or psychologist and specific types of medication. Some people just need one of those two treatments, while others need both. Some people may choose to use herbal mood support supplements to help ease their depression symptoms.

Depression looks different in different people. One person's depression treatment may be different from another's treatment. Much like the various causes of depression, everyone's recovery is different. Some people may need only a temporary round of treatment for their depression. Others might need to use medication and therapy for the rest of their lives. If you are going through treatment for your depression, do not compare your treatment to someone else's treatment. Your journey is your own.

MYTHS AND FACTS

MYTH: It's obvious when someone is depressed.

FACT: Some people who suffer from depression seem happy and cheerful when they are around friends and family. They may even be the life of the party or the most popular kid at school. Just because a person is laughing on the outside doesn't mean she is happy on the inside. Different people express their depression in different ways.

MYTH: People with depression could snap out of it if they really wanted to.

FACT: Depression is not a character flaw, it's a mental illness that deserves to be treated as such. People with depression can't just "get over it" by themselves. They need professional help, whether in the form of therapy or medication.

MYTH: Depressed people will always be depressed.

FACT: Most people who suffer from depression find relief through therapy, medication, or a combination of both. The Ganley Foundation reports that 80 to 90 percent of people respond positively to treatment for depression.

CHAPTER TWO

ALL ABOUT SELF-HARM

When a person deliberately harms her own body but is not trying to kill herself, it is called self-harm. Sometimes it is obvious when someone is self-harming. Other times, it is a well-hidden secret. Self-harm can take many forms and can look different in different people—some people might cut themselves, while others pull out their own hair.

Most people who self-harm do not want to commit suicide. They want a physical sense of relief from their depression or from a difficult event they have been through. Many people who self-harm feel compelled to continue the harmful action, even though they don't like hurting themselves. Something in their brain won't let them stop without help.

TYPES OF SELF-HARM

One of the most common types of self-harm is cutting one's skin with a knife, razor blade, or broken glass.

Although cutting is the best-known type of self-harm, there are many other ways people hurt themselves. Some people pull out their own hair, others take poisons, and some hit walls with the purpose of hurting themselves. Excessive exercising has also been called a form of self-harm, especially if the person doesn't get any health benefits from it.

Self-harm can also include scratching or pinching the skin with fingernails or objects, causing bleeding or marks on the skin. Messing with existing wounds or injuries on purpose also counts as self-harm. Even though the person

Self-harm is often a coping mechanism for dealing with powerful and overwhelming emotions.

is not creating new wounds by doing this, it is still considered to be a form of self-harm. According to the National Health Service of the United Kingdom, mental health professionals consider drug and alcohol abuse and eating disorders to be specific types of self-harm as well.

If you notice these signs in a loved one, it may be an indication that he is self-harming:

- Scars, burns, or bruises
- Random bald spots or hair loss with no medical cause
- Wearing long sleeves, even in hot weather
- Isolation from friends and loved ones
- Unpredictable or out-of-character behavior

WHY DO PEOPLE SELF-HARM?

Self-harm is complicated and can have several different causes. Some people have mental health issues that cause them to self-harm. These issues include depression as well as conditions like borderline personality disorder, bipolar disorder, and certain kinds of anxiety disorders, like obsessive-compulsive disorder or frequent panic attacks.

Other people might self-harm if they experience what psychologists call trauma. Trauma is a life-changing event that has a negative impact on someone. Incidents such as sexual abuse and assault, the death of a friend or family member, or being a victim of bullying are all things that might lead to self-harm. Major life events like moving to a new town, going through the divorce of parents, or losing a close friend can also trigger self-harm.

Many people self-harm because they don't know how to regulate, express, or understand the powerful emotions they are feeling.

SELF-HARM IN LGBTQ TEENS

The National Alliance for Mental Health reports that LGBTQ teens are at least three times more likely to experience depression and four times more likely to self-harm than their straight and cisgender peers. This is due to many factors, including a lack of support and affirmation from parents, homophobic and transphobic bullying from peers, and a lack of understanding on the part of medical professionals.

In many states, LGBTQ teens may be forced to attend "conversion therapy," an abusive practice whereby a therapist attempts to change a person's gender or sexuality. While this practice has been banned in some places, it remains legal in forty-one states, and a 2018 study by the Williams Institute estimates that twenty thousand teens will undergo conversion treatment before they turn eighteen.

"The trauma of conversion therapy can cause depression, suicidal ideation, family rejection and a whole host of horrors that children must then face without the knowledge that mental health professionals are supposed to help rather than harm," says Sam Brinton, head of advocacy and governmental affairs at The Trevor Project, an organization that provides services for LGBTQ youth. Many teens respond to these emotional traumas by engaging in self-harm as a coping mechanism.

The Trevor Project provides a wealth of resources specifically for LGBTQ teens who are dealing with depression, self-harm, and suicidal thoughts. In addition to a

(continued on the next page)

Due to social stigma and societal pressure, LGBTQ people are more likely to experience self-harm and suicidal tendencies than their straight peers. Finding a supportive community is essential.

(continued from the previous page)

twenty-four-hour-a-day hotline, the organization also offers a confidential texting service, a chat room, and a social networking site called TrevorSpace that is specifically for LGBTQ youth ages thirteen to twenty-four and their friends and allies. Find out more at www.TheTrevorProject.org.

IMPACTS OF SELF-HARM

Even though most people who self-harm do not want to kill themselves, self-harm can get out of hand and

One of the side effects of self-harm is a feeling of shame and lowered self-esteem. Some people feel ashamed of themselves immediately after they self-harm.

lead to further problems. According to the Mayo Clinic, some of the complications of self-harm can include:

- **Infection.** If a wound is deep enough or if it is not cleaned and taken care of properly, an infection can form. Infections can lead to complications, such as sepsis, other illnesses, and even more pain.
- **Worsening of anxiety or depression.** People who self-harm may experience a surge in already-intense feelings of depression or anxiety.

- **Feelings of lower self-esteem, guilt, and shame.** After self-harming, people may feel embarrassed or ashamed of their actions. These feelings can feed a vicious cycle in which increased depression leads to more self-harm.
- **Permanent scars.** Months and years of self-harm can lead to a lifetime of scars. Many people who self-harmed as teenagers find that their scars do not fade, and they have to find ways of hiding them from the rest of the world. This can also lead to an ongoing sense of shame, even after the person has stopped self-harming.
- **Fatal injury that could lead to death.** According to the National Alliance on Mental Illness, most people who self-harm do not want to die. However, if a self-injury is severe enough, it can lead to death.

GETTING HELP FOR SELF-HARM

If you are harming yourself, you may not know how to talk to your doctor about it, but it's important to find a medical professional you can trust as soon as possible. A doctor or therapist can talk with you about different ways to treat your injuries and how to find different coping strategies to help you deal with the stresses in your life, instead of self-harming. Your school counselor may be able to help you find a doctor or therapist. It's important that you like and trust your doctor or therapist. If you don't like this person, ask if you can speak with someone else instead.

When your friend has depression or is self-harming, it is important to listen to him. Although you might not have all the answers, being there for him can be helpful.

WHEN A FRIEND NEEDS HELP

If you believe a friend is self-harming, it can be hard to know how to help. Lifeline.org, a mental health website for teens, provides some suggestions:

- Encourage your friend to get help from a mental health professional, like a counselor or a doctor. Offer to go with her to her appointments if she feels scared. It can be an intimidating thing to do by oneself.

- Be calm, open, honest, and don't judge your friend. It can be hard to talk to someone about self-harm, and he may be worried about your reaction.
- Listen and be supportive of your friend's feelings. She may not want your input and advice, so try to refrain from offering it. Instead, listen to her without judging.
- Take care of yourself. Worrying about a friend's mental health can be tiring. Remember to take a break from worrying about your friend and schedule time to do something you love that will take your mind off of it. You can't help someone else if you are feeling overwhelmed yourself.

CHAPTER THREE

SUICIDE AND SUICIDAL THOUGHTS

Most people who suffer from depression get treated and go on to live full lives. That being said, suicide can be a deadly side effect of depression. Every day, 123 Americans take their own lives, according to the suicide prevention organization Overnight Walk. For those experiencing suicidal thoughts and their loved ones, it's important to understand what causes this condition and how to get help.

WHY DO PEOPLE COMMIT SUICIDE?

There is no single cause of suicide. People kill themselves for many different reasons. Depression is a top risk factor, and people who suffer from other mental illnesses, such as bipolar disorder, schizophrenia, or borderline personality disorder, are also at a high risk of suicide. Sometimes, when people with existing depression experience a tough life event, it pushes them over the edge, making their depression worse and putting them at risk for suicide. Traumatic events

Many stressful life situations can contribute to depression. Sometimes, family circumstances like parents arguing constantly or getting a divorce can lead young people to feel depressed.

such as being abused or being the victim of a violent crime can lead to a person feeling suicidal. Financial problems, family stress, and bullying can also lead to suicidal feelings.

Suicidal feelings happen when people feel overwhelmed by their own bad feelings. They feel worthless. They think that the people in their lives won't miss them and that they'd be doing people a favor by killing themselves. These feelings can be overpowering. When people don't know how to cope with these feelings, they may begin to think that suicide is their only option.

FACTS ABOUT SUICIDE

DoSomething.org is an organization that helps young people create positive changes. One of the organization's missions is to prevent suicide. DoSomething.org's suicide awareness project helps to raise awareness about suicide by providing factual information.

- Nearly thirty thousand Americans and about four thousand Canadians die by suicide each year.
- Suicide rates are the highest during the spring months (March, April, and May).

(continued on the next page)

The availablity of guns and other firearms in the United States con-tributes to its high suicide rates.

(continued from the previous page)

- **Untreated and undiagnosed depression is the number-one reason for suicide.**
- **Over 50 percent of all suicides in the United States are done with a firearm.**
- **Men and boys make up over 76 percent of all suicides, but women and girls are more prone to suicidal thoughts.**

People who are having suicidal thoughts should always seek medical care. Most people with depression and other mental illnesses can be treated successfully. Many people recover from their suicidal feelings and go on to live happy, healthy, long lives.

SUICIDAL FEELINGS CAN BE COMPLICATED

In an article titled "When You're in the Gray Area of Being Suicidal" on The Mighty, Tea Jay writes,

People think of things like suicide in such black or white terms. But much like everything else we are so quick to place into categories, being suicidal falls into a gray area for me. Sometimes, I wonder if it does for anybody else. See I can be in a really great mood, right? I could be having the best day of my life. Still, suicidal thoughts will linger. I don't have to be in a bad mood to be suicidal. I will still have those

*thoughts if I'm surrounded by the people I love,
or if I'm doing something I'm passionate about.*

Jay wrote this piece with the intention of helping people to better understand the nuances of suicidal thoughts and the internal struggles that people with suicidal thoughts experience regularly. If you are feeling suicidal, you may find your own feelings confusing and hard to explain to your friends and family. You may feel a certain way one day and a completely different way the next day. Since suicidal thoughts can be so hard to explain, it helps to find a trained professional who specializes in depression to help you work through your feelings. Ask your health care provider, a school counselor, or another trusted adult if he or she can help you find someone to talk to.

KNOW THE SIGNS

Many people think that suicide happens out of the blue and that there's nothing anyone could've done to help. In reality, most people who commit suicide give family and friends hints that go unrecognized. If you know what to look out for, you may be able to read the early warning signs and help a suicidal friend get the help she needs.

According to the State of Nevada's Office of Suicide Prevention, there are a few common signs that someone may be suicidal. These include:

- Giving away personal belongings and doing reckless or irresponsible things. People who are suicidal do not plan much for the future because they do not see themselves in it.

- Talking about wanting to die or kill themselves. This may be perceived as a way to get attention, but it is often a cry for help.
- Looking for a way to kill themselves, such as buying a gun or other weapon.
- Increased use of alcohol and drugs.
- Sleeping a lot or hardly at all.
- Talking about being a burden to other people in their lives.

HELPING A FRIEND COPE WITH SUICIDAL THOUGHTS

If you think a friend or loved one is at risk for suicide, there are many ways to help. A big way to help is listening. Your friend is more than likely overwhelmed by his intense feelings and could benefit from having someone who will listen. Try to be nonjudgmental and just listen, instead of offering your own thoughts on the situation. It can be tempting to try to minimize a person's problems by telling him it's not that bad, but this is usually not helpful. Let your friend know that he isn't alone and that you care.

You should seek the guidance of a trusted adult to help you cope with this situation. It's too much for you to handle on your own, and an adult may be able to help you find a compassionate mental health care provider for your friend to talk to.

Talking with a loved one can ease suicidal feelings. Having someone to talk to about difficult issues can make you feel better in the short term.

The most important thing to do is to make sure your friend gets the medical care or therapy that he needs. When people who feel suicidal seek help, they can be treated successfully. Many people recover from their suicidal feelings and go on to live healthy, long lives.

COPING WITH THE LOSS OF A LOVED ONE

Losing a family member or close friend is always hard, but if you lose a loved one to suicide, your emotions can be overwhelming. You will probably be in shock at first. You may blame yourself and feel that you should've recognized the signs or that you could've done something to prevent it. You may feel angry with the person who committed suicide for leaving you, or with other people in his life for not noticing the signs or not providing more support. You will probably always feel confused about why your loved one felt the need to take her life and wonder what could've prevented it.

Being left behind after a loved one's suicide can be one of the loneliest feelings, and it's important to make sure you have a support system. You may find that your friends back away because they don't know how to talk about suicide—it is a scary topic for many people. Some religious communities limit the rituals that they provide for people who die by suicide, so if you are a person who depends on your religious community for support, you may find yourself abandoned on this front, too.

Seek out people who are willing to listen and offer support. You may decide to find a therapist or counselor. Many therapists specialize in grief therapy. You may also consider joining a support group for grieving families. Finding community with other people who have gone through the same thing and can relate to your feelings can be one of the best ways to heal.

Grieving is a process, so you should give yourself the time and space you need to deal with all the intense emotions you are feeling. Don't try to rush yourself. There's no right way to grieve, so focus on what works for you. Just because somebody else grieves by visiting the gravesite of their loved one doesn't mean that you have to do that, too.

Remember that grieving takes time. There will be days when you feel OK and days when you feel you can't go on. You may never truly get over the loss of your loved one, but with the right help, you can find peace within yourself and continue to find meaning in your own life.

CHAPTER FOUR

GETTING THE HELP YOU NEED

I f you feel depressed or are having suicidal thoughts, there are many different ways of getting help. Because depression and suicidal thoughts look and feel different in different people, there is not one correct way of getting help. People who deal with suicidal thoughts should be aware that recovery can take many different forms. For some people, therapy is incredibly helpful. For others, medication might make them feel better. Many people deal with suicidal thoughts with a combination of both therapy and medication.

THERAPY

Throughout history, people have talked to one another in order to express their feelings, solve their problems, and talk through their issues. Even though it might feel funny talking to someone outside of your circle of friends or family, seeing a therapist or counselor is a normal and often extremely helpful way of working through issues.

Talking to a mental health professional can help with depression. Some people may talk to a therapist once, while others go regularly for a long period of time.

Your therapist could be a licensed counselor, psychologist, psychiatrist, social worker, or a mental health nurse. Potential therapists can be recommended to you by your primary care doctor or pediatrician. It might be scary to tell your doctor that you are going through such a tough time, but it is important that she knows. Your doctor can help you figure out the best course of treatment. You can also visit your school's counselor if you don't feel comfortable going to a health care provider.

Therapists often specialize in specific areas of psychology. Some specialize in things like anxiety,

HELP LINES

If you are not in a good place to seek help, or you do not feel confident enough to talk to someone face to face, there are several online resources, help lines, and text lines to get you the help you need. Even though you might feel lonely, you are not alone.

National Suicide Prevention Hotline
Call 1-800-273-8255
http://www.suicidepreventionlifeline.org

Many organizations help young people with depression or who self-harm. The Trevor Project helps LGBTQ teens who struggle with depression and other mental illnesses.

Crisis Text Line
Text 741741; also available on Kik and Facebook Messenger

HopeLine
Call or text 919-231-4525 or 877-235-4525
http://www.hopeline-nc.org

The Trevor Project, for LGBTQ youth
Call 866-488-7386 or text "Trevor" to 1-202-304-1200
http://www.thetrevorproject.org

Kids Help Phone (Canada)
Call 1-800-668-6868
https://kidshelpphone.ca

Youthspace.ca (Canada)
Text 778-783-0177

The American Foundation for Suicide Prevention
Call 1-888-333-2377
https://afsp.org

IMAlive Chat
http://www.imalive.org/contact-us

abuse, eating disorders and body image, phobias, and even dealing with big life events, such as going through the divorce of parents or moving to a new city. Some therapists specialize in depression and suicidal thoughts.

Most therapy sessions last about an hour. You may go to a therapist for only a few weeks, or you may continue to go on a regular basis for many years. Your therapist will give you coping strategies for how to deal with your thoughts and feelings. She may also ask you about how you react to certain situations and how you deal with intense feelings. Many therapists will give you things to work on in between sessions. These activities may include a feelings inventory, deep breathing, mindfulness techniques, and even stress relief activities like coloring or playing music.

You do not have to worry about people finding out that you go to therapy. Mental health professionals and doctors are required by law to keep their patients' information confidential. They are not allowed to share information about who they see in therapy and why they see them.

MEDICATION

Taking medication for mental health issues is a common and helpful solution for many people. Psychiatric medicines help to address your depression and suicidal thoughts by getting your brain chemistry to work better and making you feel more functional in your daily life.

There are many different types of medication for different mental health issues. These different types of medication can work with different chemicals in your brain, depending on what your symptoms are and how they present themselves. Your doctor or other health care provider can tell you which ones work best for whatever you are dealing with and can guide you through the process of taking medication for depression.

Medications used for depression are generally called antidepressants. There are several groups of antidepressants, including but not limited to SSRIs, tricyclic antidepressants, tetracyclic antidepressants, and dopamine reuptake blockers.

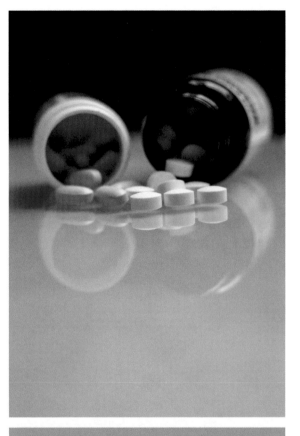

Not everyone who suffers from depression needs medication, but many others rely on it to function.

SSRIS

The most common antidepressants are SSRIs. SSRI stands for "selective serotonin reuptake inhibitor." This means these medications replace the chemical serotonin in the brain in order to "level out" emotions. SSRIs include drugs such as Prozac, Zoloft, Paxil, and Celexa.

According to the Mayo Clinic, some side effects of SSRIs can include nausea, headaches, not sleeping well, and dizziness.

TRICYCLIC ANTIDEPRESSANTS

These antidepressants were mostly used in the 1950s and 1960s. According to the Mayo Clinic, they are still effective to use for depression and suicidal thoughts, but they are not prescribed as often as SSRIs. One problem with tricyclic antidepressants is that they interact negatively with many different medications and even some foods.

TETRACYCLIC ANTIDEPRESSANTS

Tetracyclic antidepressants were heavily prescribed in the 1970s and have largely been replaced by SSRIs, which have fewer side effects. The side effects of tetracyclic antidepressants are similar to those of tricyclic antidepressants.

DOPAMINE REUPTAKE BLOCKERS

These antidepressants are also called DRIs, or dopamine reuptake inhibitors. In addition to depression, they can also be used for attention-deficit hyperactivity disorder, certain eating disorders, and other mood disorders, such as anxiety. Because of the high potential for abuse due to the main ingredients in DRIs, they are rarely prescribed for depression alone.

HERBAL SUPPLEMENTS

Some people take herbal supplements to treat their depression. One of the oldest and most popular herbal remedies for depression is St.-John's-wort. Although it is considered effective in the short term, its long-term effects are not known, according to the US Department of Health and Human Services. It is a good option for people who do not want to use a prescription medication and it is available over the counter in many supermarkets and pharmacies.

ADJUSTMENT PERIOD

No matter what medication or supplement you choose to take, there will likely be an adjustment period before the medication is fully effective. Depending on the medication and dosage, it can take anywhere from a few weeks to a month to start working at full function. Your doctor may monitor your progress and adjust your dosage. Do not feel discouraged if it takes a while before you feel the effects. Also, don't forget that different medications work for different people. If you've been taking a medication for a while and it isn't working for you, tell your doctor you'd like to try something else.

WHY IT MATTERS

It can be hard to ask for help and get the care you need when you're suffering from mental health issues, but it's the best thing you can do. Think of it this way: if you broke your leg, you wouldn't wait to call a doctor. Depression, self-harm, and suicidal feelings are just as worthy of professional care and attention as any physical ailment, and the help you get can change or even save your life. It may also inspire your friends or family members to get help for their own mental health issues.

CHAPTER FIVE

A BRIGHTER FUTURE

Mental health can be complicated—there aren't easy solutions and answers for self-harm, depression, or suicidal thoughts. That being said, there is hope. Mental illness is becoming less stigmatized than it used to be. People are becoming more open about their own struggles with depression and suicidal thoughts, which in turn leads to more people seeking treatment.

HOW CAN I PREVENT SELF-HARM, DEPRESSION, OR SUICIDAL THOUGHTS?

If you know that you have a tendency to self-harm, feel depressed, or experience suicidal thoughts, there are a few things you can do to prepare for the next time you get the urge to harm yourself. Deborah Serani, author of *Depression and Your Child*, suggests a number of coping strategies.

- **Create an emergency kit.** This can include things like a favorite stuffed animal, a journal

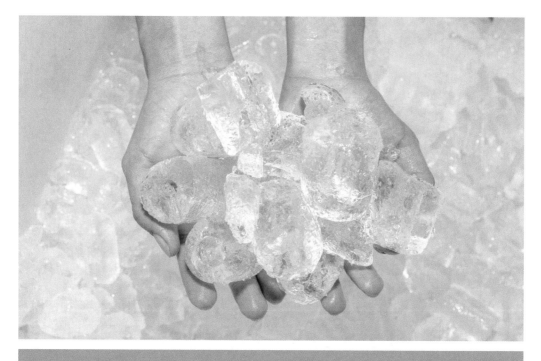

If you are tempted to self-harm, there are strategies you can learn to distract yourself. One unusual but helpful distraction method is holding ice cubes.

with markers and pens for writing about your feelings, favorite scents, photos of beloved friends and family members, or anything else you find soothing.

- **Think about positive images.** What is your favorite place? Go there in your mind by picturing it. Try this whenever you feel sad or discouraged.
- **Figure out your triggers.** Do certain people, things, or situations upset you and cause you to feel terrible? Figure out what they are and think

SOCIAL MEDIA AND MENTAL HEALTH

Although almost everyone is on social media these days, it can be damaging to your mental health if you are not careful about how you use it. According to a study by Dr. Jeff Nalin of the Anxiety and Depression Association of America, excessive social media use can lead to depression.

When people are constantly seeing what their friends are doing and comparing their friends' lives to their own, this can lead to an intense pressure to fit in and a sense of inadequacy. Social media use can

(continued on the next page)

Spending too much time on social media can negatively impact your mental health. Since social media causes you to compare yourself to others, it can lead to feelings of inadequacy.

(continued from the previous page)

also decrease real-life social skills. When teens are constantly interacting online, they forget how to focus on real-life interactions and may not develop essential social skills such as empathy. Social media is also a breeding ground for cyberbullying, and since many teens are on their phones all day and all evening, they can't escape the bullying even when they're away from the bullies. The inability to tune out of social and school life can have damaging consequences for teens' mental health.

You can still enjoy social media without developing depression. That being said, it's important to limit your time online or on apps. Social media can be addictive. If you find yourself feeling overwhelmed, sad, or stressed when you're on social media, cut back on the time you spend on various apps and platforms. This is easier said than done. You may need to put your phone out of reach, in a bag, or on a top shelf to remind yourself that you're supposed to be taking a break. You may even consider deleting some apps from your phone if you feel they are taking over your life.

about how you can deal with these triggers. Do you need to avoid them altogether, or can you adjust your response?

- **Distract yourself.** If you feel the urge to self-harm or have suicidal thoughts, find another activity to do instead. Some people tear paper, snap a rubber band, or hold ice cubes, among other techniques. Your doctor or therapist may give you some other ideas for replacement activities.

BENEFITS OF A HEALTHY LIFESTYLE

Taking care of your physical well-being can have many positive impacts on your mental health. Simple solutions such as exercising, getting enough sleep, and eating healthy meals can have huge benefits in treating depression.

Exercising is one of the best ways to stay positive or snap yourself out of a depressive period. When you exercise, your body releases endorphins—chemicals that trigger a happy feeling and give you a natural high. According to the National Institutes of Health, exercise can improve mental health by reducing anxiety and depression. It can also give people a stable outlet for working through those emotions.

Eating a healthy diet is another thing you can do to stay happy. According to the American Psychological Association, there is a clear link between a healthy diet and an improvement in mental health. Similarly, good sleep habits can set you up for healthier mental health. According to Harvard Health, "studies suggest that a good night's sleep helps foster both mental and emotional resilience."

A healthy lifestyle is not a cure for mental illness, but adopting these small habits can ease the symptoms of depression.

Finding a hobby, whether it is artistic, athletic, or anything in between, can give you something to focus on instead of depression.

SELF-CARE IS SUPER IMPORTANT

Whether you are dealing with depression, self-harm, or suicidal thoughts yourself or you are helping a friend through a tough time, it's important to make sure you take care of yourself. According to *Psychology Today*, self-care is an important part of mental health care because it gives people the opportunity to recharge and take care of themselves. Self-care gives you energy to face hard situations and makes you feel more confident in your daily life.

Much like depression, self-care looks different for different people. Some people find watching their favorite TV show relaxing, while others prefer a long run. Whatever safe activity you find relaxing or soothing counts as self-care. YourLifeCounts.org provides some suggestions for things you can do to take care of yourself:

- **Reread your favorite book or start reading a new one.** It doesn't matter what book it is— reading can take your mind off overwhelming emotions.
- **Hang out with a friend.** You don't have to talk about your mental health unless you want to. Do a fun activity together, or just sit and talk.
- **Sit outside and just listen.** The quiet of nature can be relaxing and soothing. You don't have to go on a long, difficult hike. Just sit outside and relax.
- **Take a walk.** Even a short walk can be a great way to recharge. If you start feeling overwhelmed, a walk can refocus your energy.
- **Yoga.** This ancient practice is not only an effective exercise, but many people find it to be incredibly relaxing.
- **Go for a run or play your favorite sport.** If you have a favorite sport or active hobby, it can help with your physical and mental health.
- **Write.** It feels good to get your emotions out of your head and onto a computer screen or a paper journal. Write whatever comes into your head. You don't need to share it with anyone.

Being around animals can have positive health benefits. Some studies have traced lowered blood pressure and increased feelings of overall happiness to spending regular time around animals.

- **Make art, whether it's painting, photography, or something else.** Creative expression can be great for mental health.
- **Watch a favorite movie.** Particularly if the movie is comforting, it can be soothing during a rough time.
- **Do an activity that comforts or soothes you.** Some ideas include playing video games, listening to music, doing a sport or other physical activity, cooking, coloring, or meditating.
- **Talk to a trusted friend or family member.** Sometimes, just talking to someone about a problem or concern can make things better.

- **Play with a pet or a friend's pet.** According to WebMD, having a pet has health benefits. Some of these benefits include lower blood pressure, decreased risk of heart disease, and a lower rate of depression and anxiety.
- **Think of your own personal goals or plans for the future.** Write them down so you can refer back to them. This can give you inspiration for the future.
- **Take a nap.** Rest can be great for stress relief, especially if you aren't getting enough sleep at night.
- **Watch funny or inspiring videos on YouTube.** Taking a break to watch something comforting or hilarious can provide you with a welcome sense of relief. For at least a little while, you are focused on something besides depression.

YOU'RE WORTH IT

It takes courage to admit that you need help, especially for self-harm, depression, or suicidal thoughts. Although it's not an easy process, and it may take a while for you to start to feel better, seeking help for your mental health problems is well worth it. Remember, the world needs your unique voice, thoughts, experiences, and actions. Think of all the things you can achieve in your life. You are wanted and needed, and you deserve to get the help you need when you are facing mental health challenges. Acknowledging the issue and getting help is more than half the battle, and your future self will thank you.

10 GREAT QUESTIONS TO ASK A DOCTOR

1. How can I decide what treatment is best for my depression/self-harm/suicidal thoughts?
2. How can I find a therapist I like and trust?
3. What can I do when I feel like harming myself?
4. What can I do when I feel suicidal?
5. What is my official diagnosis?
6. What are the side effects of the medication I'm taking?
7. How long does this medication take to start working?
8. When should I go to the hospital or emergency room?
9. I don't want to take prescription medication. What are my other options?
10. In addition to therapy and/or medicine, what can I do to help improve my mental health?

bipolar disorder A brain disorder characterized by extreme changes in mood and activity levels.

depression A serious mood disorder that affects a person's ability to function in daily life.

diagnosis Identifying an illness or condition based on the symptoms.

empathy The quality of relating to how other people feel and showing compassion for their circumstances.

functional Being able to cope with everyday tasks.

mental health Emotional well-being; how a person feels and acts.

phobia An irrational fear of something specific.

postpartum depression Feelings of sadness and anxiety experienced after giving birth.

psychiatrist A medical doctor who deals with mental, emotional, and behavioral issues.

risk factor A situation or incident that increases risk.

seasonal affective disorder A condition characterized by feeling depressed during the winter months.

self-harm The act of injuring oneself physically to cope with emotional pain.

suicidal feelings The desire to take one's own life.

suicide The act of taking one's own life.

trauma A life-changing event or circumstance that has an ongoing negative impact on a person.

treatment The process of addressing and healing an illness or condition.

FOR MORE INFORMATION

American Foundation for Suicide Prevention
120 Wall Street, 29th Floor
New York, NY 10005
(1-888) 333-2377
Website: https://afsp.org
Facebook, Twitter, and Instagram: @AFSPnational
This organization provides a wealth of information and
   support services relating to suicide prevention and
   mental health. There are local chapters in many cities.

Canadian Association for Suicide Prevention
PO Box 53082, RPO Rideau Centre
Ottawa, ON K1N 1C5
Canada
(613) 702-4446
Website: https://suicideprevention.ca
Facebook: @ CanadianAssociationforSuicidePrevention
Twitter: @CASP_CA
This organization provides resources for people experi-
   encing depression and suicidal thoughts, as well as
   links to crisis centers across Canada.

DoSomething.org
19 West 21st Street, 8th Floor
New York, NY 10010
(212) 254-2390
Website: https://dosomething.org
Facebook, Twitter, and Instagram: @dosomething

This organization seeks to create positive change in the lives of young people by providing teens with volunteer opportunities, creating positive social media campaigns, and raising awareness for issues such as suicide prevention.

HOPE Squad
Website: https://hopesquad.com
Facebook: @hopecanchangeeverything
Twitter: @HopeSquads
This organization operates clubs in many high schools and middle schools across North America. Contact them to start a club at your school.

IMAlive
Website: https://www.imalive.org/contact-us
Facebook: @IMAlive
Twitter: @_IMAlive
Instagram: @imalivechatline
IMAlive is an online-only chat service on which users can talk about mental health issues or life events.

National Institute of Mental Health
6001 Executive Boulevard, Room 6200, MSC 9663
Bethesda, MD 20892
(866) 615-6464
Website: https://www.nimh.nih.gov
Facebook and Twitter: @nimhgov
This US-based research organization provides comprehensive information about research on all kinds of mental health issues.

Native Youth Crisis Hotline
(877) 209-1266
Website: http://youarenotalonenetwork.org/in-crisis
This crisis hotline is specifically for First Nations youth
in Canada.

Suicide Prevention Lifeline
50 Broadway
New York, NY 10004
(800) 273-8255
Website: https://suicidepreventionlifeline.org
Facebook, Twitter, and Instagram: @800273TALK
This national network of crisis centers offers a hotline
and resources for people experiencing suicidal
thoughts and their loved ones.

The Trevor Project
PO Box 69232
West Hollywood, CA 90069
(866) 488-7386
Website: https://www.thetrevorproject.org
Facebook: @TheTrevorProject
Twitter and Instagram: @TrevorProject
The Trevor Project provides a hotline, texting service, and
social media network for LGBTQ youth who are experi-
encing depression or having suicidal thoughts.

Angelici, Sharon K. *Dear Kane; What I Wish We Would Have Said.* Denver, CO: Write with Light Publications, 2016.

Beam, Linda, and Donalyn Powell. *Stepping Up: Finding Healing for Your Life and Hope for the Future.* New York, NY: Morgan James Publishing, 2017.

Bleuel, Amy. *Project Semicolon: Your Story Isn't Over.* New York, NY: HarperCollins, 2017.

Bornstein, Kate. *Hello Cruel World: 101 Alternatives to Suicide for Teens, Freaks, and Other Outlaws.* New York, NY: Seven Stories Press, 2006.

Davis, Geoffrey A., and Judy Davis. *Warning Signs: A Parenting Guide for Discovering If Your Teen Is at Risk for Depression, Addiction, or Suicide.* Charleston, SC: CreateSpace, 2015.

Fagan, Kate. *What Made Maddy Run: The Secret Struggles and Tragic Death of an All-American Teen.* Boston, MA: Little, Brown, and Company, 2017.

Galas, Judith C., and Richard E. Nelson. *The Power to Prevent Suicide: A Guide for Teens Helping Teens.* Golden Valley, MN: Free Spirit Publishing, 2006.

Goldsmith, Connie. *Understanding Suicide: A National Epidemic.* Minneapolis, MN: Twenty-First Century Books, 2016.

Itou, Tina. *Suicide Prevention: The Ultimate Guide to Suicide Prevention.* Amazon Digital Services, LLC, 2014.

Kohnen, Kara. *13 Reasons 'Why Am I Going to Counseling?' For Teens: A Guide for Teens Starting Counseling.* San Diego, CA: independently published, 2017.

American Psychiatric Association. *Diagnostic and Statistical Manual of Mental Disorders.* 5th ed. Washington, D.C.: American Psychiatric Publishing, 2013.

Castillo, Stephanie. "Am I Depressed? The Types of People More Prone to Depression." Medical Daily, August 22, 2014. http://www.medicaldaily.com /am-i-depressed-types-people-more-prone -depression-299286.

Cherry, Kendra. *The Everything Psychology Book.* 2nd ed. Avon, MA: Adams Media, 2010.

Gluck, Samantha. "Self Injury, Self Harm Statistics, and Facts." Healthy Place, August 26, 2016. https://www .healthyplace.com/abuse/self-injury/self-injury-self -harm-statistics-and-facts.

Janssen, Mary Beth. *The Book of Self-Care: 200 Ways to Refresh, Restore, and Rejuvenate.* New York, NY: Sterling Ethos Publishing, 2017.

Jay, Tea. "When You're in the Gray Area of Being Suicidal." The Mighty, March 22, 2016. https://the mighty.com/2016/03/when-you-feel-suicidal-but -dont-want-to-die.

Mayo Clinic Staff. "Depression and Mental Illness Information Page." Mayo Clinic. Retrieved February 27, 2018. https://www.mayoclinic.org/diseases-conditions /depression/symptoms-causes/syc-20356007.

Mayo Clinic Staff. "Suicide Grief: Coping After a Loved One's Suicide." Mayo Clinic, October 2, 2015. https:// www.mayoclinic.org/healthy-lifestyle/end-of-life /in-depth/suicide/art-20044900.

Nalin, Jeff. "Social Media and Teen Depression: The Two Go Hand-In-Hand." Anxiety and Depression Association of America. Retrieved March 4, 2018. https://adaa.org/learn-from-us/from-the-experts/blog-posts/consumer/social-media-and-teen-depression-two-go-hand#.

National Institute of Mental Health. "Suicide Prevention." Mental Health Information. Retrieved March 1, 2018. https://www.nimh.nih.gov/health/topics/suicide-prevention/index.shtml.

National Institutes of Health. "St. John's Wort and Depression: In Depth." January 4, 2018. https://nccih.nih.gov/health/stjohnswort/sjw-and-depression.htm.

Nock, Matthew K. *The Oxford Handbook of Suicide and Self-Injury.* Oxford, England: Oxford University Press, 2014.

Serani, Deborah. *Depression and Your Child: A Guide for Parents and Caregivers.* Boulder, CO: Rowman and Littlefield, 2015.

State of Nevada. "Office of Suicide Prevention Homepage." Retrieved February 27, 2018. http://suicideprevention.nv.gov.

Weir, Kristen. "The Exercise Effect." American Psychological Association, December 2011. http://www.apa.org/monitor/2011/12/exercise.aspx.

World Health Organization. "Mental Health: Suicide Prevention." September 1, 2017. http://www.who.int/mental_health/suicide-prevention/en.

Wylie, John V. *Diagnosing and Treating Mental Illness: A Guide for Physicians, Nurses, Patients, and Their Families.* Spokane, WA: Demers Books, 2010.

M

medication, 6, 15–16, 17, 36, 40–43, 54
mental health, 4, 6, 12, 14, 19, 20, 21, 25–26, 32, 37, 40, 44, 47–48, 49–53, 54
mental health professional, 6, 19, 21, 25, 32, 37, 40
military, 5, 11

P

persistent depressive disorder, 8
phobia, 21, 39
postpartum depression, 8
psychiatrist, 37, 40

R

recovery, 16, 30, 33, 36
risk factor, 27

S

scars, 20, 24
schizophrenia, 14, 27
seasonal affective disorder, 8
self-care, 10, 26, 49–51
self-harm, 4, 6, 7, 15, 18–20, 21, 22–26, 44, 45, 48, 50, 53, 54
signs, 6–7, 9–10, 20, 31, 34
sleep, 10, 32, 42, 49, 53

social media, 4, 47–48
SSRIs, 41–42
stigma, 6, 7, 12, 13–14, 45
St.-John's-wort, 43
stress, 5, 11, 24, 28, 40, 48, 53
suicidal feelings, 28, 30, 33, 44
suicidal ideation, 21
suicidal thoughts, 7, 21, 36, 39, 42, 45, 48, 50, 53, 54
suicide, 4, 6, 15, 18, 27–28, 29–30, 30–34, 38–39
support, 12, 15, 21, 26, 34
symptoms, 7, 9–10, 15, 41, 49

T

taboo, 6, 7, 13
tetracyclic antidepressants, 41–42
therapy, 6, 15–16, 17, 21, 33–34, 36, 40, 54
trauma, 5, 8, 10, 20, 21, 27
treatment, 4, 6, 7, 9, 14–16, 17, 21, 37, 45, 54
Trevor Project, 21–22, 39
tricyclic antidepressants, 41–42
triggers, 8, 20, 46, 48–49

ABOUT THE AUTHOR

Erin Pack-Jordan holds a BA in history and a master's degree in education from the University of North Texas. She has taught high school social studies and debate for several years and hopes to eventually become a school psychologist. She lives with her family in Salt Lake City, Utah.

PHOTO CREDITS